W9-AHG-909

First Cookbooks

A Football COOKBOOK

Simple Recipes for Kids

by Sarah L. Schuette

CAPSTONE PRESS
a capstone imprint

First Facts is published by Capstone Press,
1710 Roe Crest Drive, North Mankato, Minnesota 56003.
www.capstonepub.com

Books published by Capstone Press are manufactured with paper
containing at least 10 percent post-consumer waste.

Library of Congress Cataloging-in-Publication Data
Schuette, Sarah L., 1976–
  A football cookbook : simple recipes for kids / by Sarah L. Schuette.
    p. cm.— (First facts. First cookbooks)
  Includes bibliographical references and index.
  Summary: "Provides instructions and step-by-step photos for making a variety of simple snacks and
drinks with a football theme"—Provided by publisher.
  ISBN 978-1-4296-7620-5 (library binding)
  1. Snack foods—Juvenile literature. 2. Cooking—Juvenile literature. 3. Football—Juvenile literature.
    I. Title.
  TX740.S32563 2012
  641.5'3—dc23   2011030311

Editorial Credits

Christine Peterson editor; Ashlee Suker, designer; Sarah Schuette, photo stylist; Marcy Morin, studio
    scheduler; Kathy McColley production specialist

Photo Credits

All images Capstone Studio/Karon Dubke except:
Dreamstime/R. Gino Santa Maria (football helmet), cover

The author dedicates this book to her Uncle Frank Hilgers.

Printed in the United States of America in North Mankato, Minnesota.
102011
006405CGS12

Table of Contents

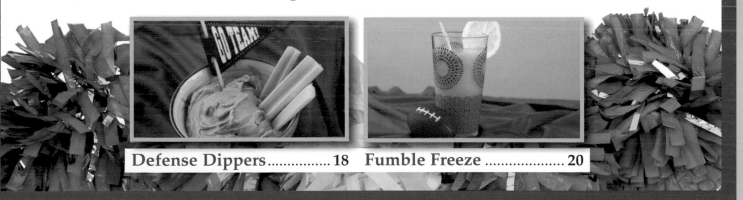

Punt, Pass, Cook!

Whoosh! The **quarterback** sends the ball soaring. Thud! A **lineman** slams a receiver to the turf. The crowd roars with excitement. Football players and fans work up an **appetite** on game day.

Want some snacks for the big game? Don't **fumble** around the kitchen. Study your recipes like a game plan. Look in the cupboards for what you need. Need some help on the field? Ask an adult coach to help.

Take a time-out to wash your hands. And remember to clean up at the end of the game. You'll be sure to score extra points with your team.

Metric Conversion Chart	
United States	**Metric**
¼ teaspoon	1.2 mL
½ teaspoon	2.5 mL
1 teaspoon	5 mL
1 tablespoon	15 mL
¼ cup	60 mL
⅓ cup	80 mL
½ cup	120 mL
⅔ cup	160 mL
¾ cup	175 mL
1 cup	240 mL
1 ounce	30 gms

Tools

Football players need the right equipment before heading on the field. So do you. Use this handy guide to track down the tools you'll need.

blender—a small electric appliance with a tall plastic or glass container and metal blades

butter knife—an eating utensil often used to spread ingredients or cut soft food

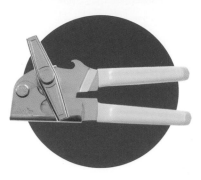

can opener—a tool used to open metal cans

cutting board—a wooden or plastic board used when slicing or chopping foods

dry-ingredient measuring cups—round cups with handles used for measuring dry ingredients

measuring spoons—spoons with small deep scoops used to measure both wet and dry ingredients

microwave-safe bowl—a bowl made of plastic or glass that is used to heat ingredients in a microwave

mixing bowl—a sturdy bowl used for mixing ingredients

pizza cutter—a round knife that spins on a handle as you slice

pot holders—a thick, heavy fabric cut into a square or circle that is used to handle hot items.

strainer—a bowl-shaped tool with holes in the sides and bottom used for draining liquid off food

Techniques

drain—to remove the liquid from something

mash—to crush with a fork

measure—to take a specific amount of something

scoop—to lift or pick up something

spread—to cover a surface with something

sprinkle—to scatter something in small drops or bits

stir—to mix something by moving a spoon around in it

Crowd-Pleasing Pizza

Nothing says game day like pizza! Try this veggie-packed pizza at your next football party. It's sure to score a touchdown with friends.

Serves 4

Ingredients:

- 1 pre-baked pizza crust (7-inch)
- 1 8-ounce tub of fat-free cream cheese
- ¼ cup chopped fresh broccoli
- ¼ cup shredded carrots
- ¼ cup shredded cheddar cheese
- 6 grape tomatoes

Tools:

- small plate
- spoon
- dry-ingredient measuring cups
- three small bowls
- butter knife
- cutting board
- pizza cutter

TIP:
Not a broccoli fan? You can make this pizza using any of your favorite vegetables.

1 Lay pizza crust on plate. Using a spoon, spread cream cheese on crust.

2 Measure broccoli, shredded carrots, and cheese into small bowls. Top crust with vegetables.

3 With an adult's help, slice each tomato in half on a cutting board. Place the tomatoes on the pizza.

4 Sprinkle cheese on top.

5 With a pizza cutter, cut pizza into wedges and serve.

Quarterback Snack

The quarterback sneaks a snack to keep sharp during game time. Munch on this tasty snack mix between plays, and you'll be snacking like a pro.

Serves 2

Ingredients:
- 1 cup cinnamon-flavored cereal
- 1 cup dried apple pieces
- 1 cup mixed nuts
- 1 cup golden raisins

Tools:
- large mixing bowl
- dry-ingredient measuring cups
- spoon
- zip-top bag

1 In a large mixing bowl, measure and add cereal and apple pieces.

2 Measure mixed nuts and raisins. Add to bowl.

3 Mix ingredients with a spoon. Store in a zip-top bag for snacking during the game.

TIP:
This snack mix uses pistachios, almonds, and cashews, but you can use any of your favorite nuts.

FOOTBALL

Touchdown Chili

When your team is ahead at **halftime**, fuel up on this hearty chili. Your friends will cheer like you just scored a touchdown!

Serves 4-6

Ingredients:
- 1 15-ounce can diced tomatoes
- 1 15-ounce can black beans
- 1 15-ounce can chili beans
- 1 15-ounce can navy beans
- 1 7-ounce can corn
- ½ cup shredded carrots
- 1 teaspoon onion flakes
- ⅛ teaspoon garlic powder
- ⅛ teaspoon chili powder
- ¼ cup ketchup
- ¼ teaspoon sugar

Tools:
- can opener
- large microwave-safe bowl
- strainer
- dry-ingredient measuring cups
- spoon
- measuring spoons
- paper towel
- pot holders

TIP: Don't want to miss a minute of the game? Cook your chili in a slow cooker for four to six hours. Stir once each hour.

1 Use a can opener to open the tomatoes, beans, and corn.

2 Pour tomatoes and chili beans into a large, microwave-safe bowl.

3 With a strainer, drain the liquid off the corn, navy beans, and black beans. Add beans and corn to bowl.

4 Measure and add shredded carrots to the large bowl. Stir.

5 Measure onion flakes, garlic powder, chili powder, ketchup, and sugar. Add to the large bowl. Mix well with spoon.

6 Cover bowl with paper towel. Microwave chili for two minutes. With pot holders, remove bowl and stir. Heat chili for another two minutes.

Goalpost Guacamole

An **avocado** looks like a football, but it tastes much better. **Rally** the crowd, and score big with this delicious dip.

Serves 4

Ingredients:

- 1 avocado
- 2 teaspoons lime juice
- 1 teaspoon chopped freeze-dried onion
- 1 teaspoon minced garlic
- 1 teaspoon cilantro
- ¼ teaspoon salt
- 2 teaspoons pico de gallo
- tortilla chips for dipping

Tools:

- knife
- cutting board
- spoon
- mixing bowl
- measuring spoons
- fork

TIP:

Save your pit, and you can grow your own avocados. Stick four toothpicks in each side and let the pit hang in a glass of water. You will have roots in about six weeks. Plant the pit in a pot, and watch it grow!

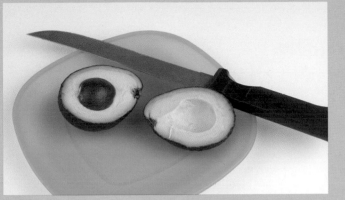

1 With an adult's help, cut one avocado in half on a cutting board. Remove the pit.

2 Using a spoon, scoop out the soft, green insides from the skin. Add avocado to bowl.

3 Measure lime juice, and add to bowl.

4 Measure onion, garlic, cilantro, salt, and pico de gallo. Add to avocado.

5 Mash mixture with a fork. If you want it less chunky, add one more teaspoon of lime juice.

6 Serve dip with tortilla chips.

Time-Out Tacos

Take a time-out with these fish tacos. The whole crowd is sure to want one. Better hold on to your helmet. Here they come!

Serves 1

Ingredients:
- 2 frozen fish sticks
- 1 hard taco shell
- 1 lime wedge
- 2 teaspoons pico de gallo
- ⅛ cup shredded cheddar cheese
- ⅛ cup shredded lettuce
- 1 teaspoon fat-free sour cream

Tools:
- microwave-safe plate
- spoon
- dry-ingredient measuring cups
- measuring spoons

1 Place fish sticks on plate. Microwave fish for two minutes or until fully cooked. Let stand for one minute.

2 Add fish sticks to taco shell.

3 Squeeze the lime wedge over the fish sticks.

4 Spoon pico de gallo on top of the fish.

5 Measure cheese and lettuce, and sprinkle on top of taco.

6 Top off with sour cream.

Defense Dippers

Defense! Defense! In football the defense holds the line and keeps the other team from scoring. Like a defense, this snack will stop hunger in its tracks.

Serves 1

Ingredients:
- 3 tablespoons peanut butter
- 1 tablespoon honey
- ¼ teaspoon soy sauce
- ¼ teaspoon sesame oil
- ¼ teaspoon water
- celery sticks

Tools:
- measuring spoons
- small bowl
- spoon

 1 Measure and add peanut butter and honey to a small bowl.

2 Measure soy sauce, sesame oil, and water. Add to bowl.

3 Stir mixture together until smooth.

4 Serve with celery sticks for dipping.

TIP:
Try spreading the dip on slices of cucumber.

Fumble Freeze

Fumbles can change a football game in a snap. You might want to wear gloves to hang onto this cool treat. You don't want to cause a fumble in the kitchen!

Serves 2

Ingredients:
- 1 15-ounce can apricot halves
- 2 tablespoons sugar
- 1 tablespoon lemon juice

Tools:
- can opener
- strainer
- zip-top bag
- blender
- measuring spoons
- 2 glasses

1 Open can of apricots with can opener. Using a strainer, drain the juice from the fruit.

2 Place apricots in zip-top bag. Seal the bag, and put it in the freezer for two to three hours.

3 Put frozen apricots in the blender.

4 Measure and add sugar and lemon juice to the blender.

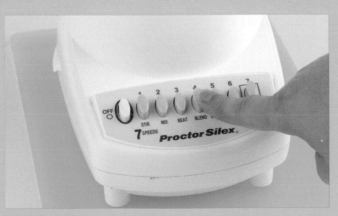

5 With an adult's help, cover blender and press blend button. Blend for one minute or until smooth.

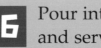

6 Pour into glasses and serve.

Glossary

appetite (AP-uh-tite)—a natural desire for food

avocado (ah-vuh-KAH-doh)—a green or black pear–shaped fruit with a tough skin and creamy, light green pulp inside

defense (di-FENS)—the team that tries to stop points from being scored; the defense is the team that doesn't have the ball

fumble (FUHM-buhl)—to drop the football while running with it

halftime (HAF-time)—a short break in the middle of a football game

lineman (LINE-muhn)—one of the football players in the line

quarterback (KWOR-tur-bak)—a football player who leads the offense by passing the ball or handing it off to a runner

rally (RAL-ee)—to join together to support a person or thing

Read More

Gregory, Josh. *Chef*. Cool Careers. Ann Arbor, Mich.: Cherry Lake Pub., 2011.

Karmel, Annabel. *Cook It Together*. New York, DK Pub., 2009.

Schuette, Sarah L. *A Superhero Cookbook: Simple Recipes for Kids*. First Cookbooks. Mankato, Minn.: Capstone Press, 2012.

Internet Sites

FactHound offers a safe, fun way to find Internet sites related to this book. All of the sites on FactHound have been researched by our staff.

Here's all you do:

Visit *www.facthound.com*

Type in this code: 9781429676205

Super-cool stuff! Check out projects, games and lots more at **www.capstonekids.com**

Index